POETICALLY PUT

POETICALLY PUT

A. Drayton

A Conscious Collective

PALMETTO
PUBLISHING
Charleston, SC
www.PalmettoPublishing.com

Hardcover ISBN: 9798822962187
Paperback ISBN: 9798822962194
eBook ISBN: 9798822962200

*This Book is Dedicated to Mary (Dolly) Drayton
Gone too soon but never forgotten* 💔

Table of Contents

Hollow Gestures

Hollow gestures disguised as pleasantries hides the truth
and intent that we never see

Good morning good morning but do we really mean it or is
it not to be rude or just merely convenient

If we really feel it's such a good morning would we mumble
it out or say it while we're yawning

I get it i do it's more of a gesture to break the awkward
silence and alleviate the pressure

Because if we stand under this banner of mean what you
say and say what you mean and real men don't play

We'll find our world to be a much colder place divided by
views economics and race

So continue the gestures half hearted or not we know who
we are and we know who we're not

If for nothing else it's a form of respect that gives us a
starting point so we can better connect

That's not who they are

We see them in the streets and in the alley ways and in front
of our local stores

Some feel disgust or lack of trust as they stand there
holding the doors

Now some are sympathetic and feel they'll regret it if they
don't give a dollar or two

Some say they'll only use it to buy drugs and that;s the
reason that they don't do

Your reasons are your reasons and that's what it is no
reason to debate or spar

But their situation is just that a situation but that's not
who they are

A bad break a bad mistake or even just a string of bad luck
a fall from grace can put you in this place and without no
help you'll be stuck

A horrible fate a tragic state for anyone to have to be in and
if it were you you would hope that people would treat you
like a human beings

Cause once you're labled homeless people see a title and no longer feel it involves them they no longer see you as their fellow man more of a systemic problem

So when you're out in the streets or in the stores or just out driving your car just remember their situation is just a situation but that's not who they are

Higher self

The daily grind can pressure the mind with unrelenting force and despite your efforts or code of ethics it can knock you off your course

How many have claimed to carry the flame on the path to true divinity only to find them standing in line on a path laid by the enemy

See we lose our way we fall we stray but that's all a part of livin it's the landscape for man's fate for this precious gift we've been given

We navigate the love & hate the trials and tribulations we work with haste to keep the paste yet still we seek the patience

See none of us are perfect and all of this is for a reason we must go through the changes as does nature does the seasons

And on this road we acquire a load an abundance of mental wealth to our sub reality which is spirituality on the road to our higher self

Charlies Changing

Charlies changing and i don't know why he use to be the
life of the party he was the one that when the cowboys won
he would want to hug everybody
Always quick to chat about scores & stats and what they're
going to do this year and if it was at your place you can
depend on Chuck coming through with a 12 pack of beer
He was always present always [pleasant wit a warm and
inviting smile and if you seemed troubled or a little bit
down he would sit and chat for a while
But as time went on Charlie started to change and his
light slowly started to go dim and the general consensus
of those that new him was the same he just wasn't him
He became separated and more isolated to the point that he
wasn't himself and as rumors goes there was marital woes
and something going on with his health
See a friend of charlie had spoke to his wife who said
life at home was terrible between his radical views and
swings in moods see charlie had become unbearable
He became fixated on political news and it changed his
whole demeana from outlets that wreak hate to conspiring
deep state he was baptised inside this arena
Things only got seedier when he turned to social media
with no one there to consult there he met up with a team
of obnoxious extreme that strongly resembled a cult
He started dressing different no longer speaking and even
let his hair grow out there was a conversation about the
state of the nation and Charlie begin to shout

About immigration and how they're taking our country
and nobodys taking my guns the loose mentality around
sexuality and what it was doing to his sons
He stormed out of the lunch room made his way to his car
and we didn't see Charlie for days those who witnessed the
explosion stood ther frozon perplexexed and somewhat in
a daze
About a week went by no sight of Charlie and everyone
was genuinely concerned we started pressing and asking the
tough questions more importantly what did we learn
One day at the job on the way back from lunch there was
cop cars in front of the building the scene was mobbed as
the secretary sobbed and screamed OMG he killed them
Decked in military garm ready to inflict harm charlie made
his way back to the plant
Where he kicked in the door and let the AK roar no pause
no flaws no rants
I often think about what took place and how much more
we could have done had we intervened the moment we seen
long before the hatred begun
So i'll say this to you if you have a friend like charlie this is
what you do for him talk to him hug him tell him you love
him but don't let his light go dim

Control

Control is something we think we have but it's really just
an illusion we try our best to weather the test of chaos and
confusion
Day by day we forge away by knowing exactly what to
say or what to do or how to do it in my way i'm going
through it
Perseverance is in his eyes he's crossed his Tee's and dot
his I's
Laser focus in the redline called the meetings and made the
deadlines proficient yes but not much wiser his life exist in
a organizer
Cause he had blinders he never saw he didn't factor in
Murphy's law or didn't listen to the senseless rumors that
the universe had a sense of humor
For all your gains there will be some loss the prominent
boss but it comes with a cost
He swiped birthdays for workdays forgot anniversaries
don't forget to get the kids from the nursery
Longer hours the kids getting older the bed seems bigger
and much more colder
The career is demanding more of your talent your life is
slipping and you lost your balance
Each side requiring more & more you're the rope in a tug
of war
Try to hold on and just don't break because everything you
worked to build is at stake
The house the wife the kids it's all there your career is your
mistress and your wife won't share

You try to save it but divorce is eminent and you and your
wife don't share the same sentiment things get ugly and
now there's a grudge and the control you once had now lies
wit the judge
As he inhales deeply and thumb through the files in the
doom & gloom court room of no smiles
He said from what i can see you're a pretty big boss but for
all your gains there's gonna be some lost

Mystic Sea

I'm drawn to you and i don't know why it's like a deep
down inner calling you encompass the world the mother of
pearls even catch the stars when falling
I stand in awe of your infinite power the ability to soothe
but also devour
We study your tides your waves your flows and still there's
so much that we don't know
You massage the grounds of coastal towns and paint a
picture of tranquility but when your mood change you
become deranged with no mercy or civility
You reside in the tropics with the hearts & souls but also with
the glaciers in the frigid cold you've witnessed the presence of
the young & old imagine the secrets that you must hold
We cruise your surface and all of it's splendor but know
nothing of your depths i walk your sands holding my lovers
hand and you wash away my steps
You were always here mystique in might even before it was
said let there be light
And when we got cocky about what we can do you took
Atlantis and the Titanic too
Just to tell us or remind us that we're just not that big as to
tell us you are a forest and we're just a twig
So i am humbled in your presence and gleeful in your
leisure fun in the sun or the ultimate plunge we have no
control of neither
Your rip tides rip lives from love ones without a warrant
Tsunamis come on land and take our plans within it
torrents

Only the heavens stars moon sun can exist up above you
seduce us but its useless cause i still don't love you
I know your ways i know your deeds i know the devastation
the place was yours from shore to shore long before our
creation
Perhaps we're the guest that made a mess and you're ready
for us to leave polluted the seas cut down the trees and it's
hard for us to breath
Our destructive ways obstruct your waves and disrupt the
natural order the righteous road is a heavier load so we take
the path that's shorter
Perhaps you're just in showing us the back hand of
disobedience countless examples of how you trample but
for some reason we're just not heeding this
We continue to defy and perpetuate the lie that what
we do don't matter despite the intensity of storms that's
unseasonably warm and all the scientific data
But i get it now i truly do dare i say that i understand
you've been deemed the guardian or should i say protector
over air see and land it is your job to set the boundaries that
keeps us all in check and although we've been granted this
fruitful planet there must also be respect so i salute you in
fulfilling this task in perhaps what you were born to you
And perhaps it's my admiration for what you do that keeps
me drawn to you

When we Love

When we love we give so much that it leaves us incomplete
our hearts our minds our focus our time is all gathered in a
way that's unique

And our significant other friend or lover the recipient of
these jewels play a significant role in our hearts and souls in
whatever path we chose

When we love it's a spiritual high we feel shields us from
any harm you're my diamond my pearl and all's right with
the world when i'm holding you in my arms

And when we're apart my yearning heart longs to be
completed your smile your touch your enchanting clutch i
want i love i need it

When you're near you become the light that makes the rest
of the world seem dim i'm like the restless explorer who's
traveled the world and finally found his gem

The admiration the appreciation nothing can feel more
better and when we occupy a space with a loving embrace i
want it to last forever

I've entrusted you with the keys to my heart in hopes that
you'll hold it sacred

You have the power to groom and watch it bloom but you also have the power to break it

And for some reason there was a change in season and you chose to do the latter where you reduced me to a state of hurt & hate to the point wher nothing else mattered

You've taken my purpose and deemed me worthless and ripped my heart right out my chest my eyes are teary my heart nis weary but my mind won't let me rest

This overwhelming pain inside has made me a victim of shame & pride and i need my inner strength to see me through
My friends say hey yuo'll be alright i said i know i will just not tonight i need some time to process this thing through It's hard to stay focus and just move on with the state that my soul is in but i know through self care and constant prayer eventually i'll be whole again but i must walk away i can't beg you to stay no matter what i endure because i love you boo i swear i do but i must love myself more

What will we say

What will we say when it's all said and done when we're
bloodied and battered and nobody won

And those who escaped the gun fell victim to the sword and
we find ourselves sitting at the feet of the lord

What will we say to the greatest of great how we shed
his grace and descended into hate and the the lessons he
bestowed we chose to ignore while our finest minds design
weapons of war

What will we say of the distribution of wealth and how if
you don't have it you can't maintain your health how one
can feed a community with what he wears on his wrist on
the same damn planet where famine exist

What will we say of selfish deeds individuality fueled
by greed where brotherly love is just a facade where we
abandoned the first commandment by making money a god

What will we say of the dwindling hope that one might
feel at the end of his rope where every giving sunday we're
reciting your quotes where mega church's get used just for
tallying votes

What will we say of the legion of poor the homeless the sick
and the rich wants more where nations get bombed for the

actions of some and they're begging for refuge and nobody
comes

What will we say
What will he say

Man succumbs to Man

Give man food give man water give man shelter to live give man companion of deep understanding and anything else you can give
Give man security give man purpose and anything his heart desires and man will choose war hate greed lust brimstone & fire
Give man land that he commands with trees that bare fruit & cattle man will choose nation confrontation tyranny bloodshed in battle
Give man riches beyond his needs with a treasure trove that's immense and he'll slay his neighbor and take his land and call it self defense
To kill is enate it's a kin to hate and very much a part of man's affliction we've grown thick skin to hatred & sin to the point where it's become an addiction
But if we stepped out of the pages of the story being written just so we can better understand we'll see the title of the book in big bold print that reads **Man succumbs to Man!**

Look To The Boarders

Look to the borders when things seem tough and you've lost
sight of what you poses witness the misery the desperation the
laborious faces of stress

Try to imagine the life they lived and all that it took to
come i'm sure it fall short of what you see on resorts and
what they are running from

It's easy to take for granted the lives we have because it's
all that we've ever known and the criminalization of the
immigrant population is all we're ever shown

This political football gets kicked back and forth so we
forget what we're actually seeing cause once we focus on
titles it no longer seems vital that we're speaking of human
beings

Citizenship, civil liberties and an abundance of
opportunities freedom of speech, freedom of religion none
of these things are new to me

But to those who come it's everything and literally worth
dying for because the ideal of the american dream promises
so much more

Through the desert and over the walls and even the
treacherous waters when you start to feel bad about what
you don't have stop and just look to the borders

I still believe

Optimism has been hunted down bludgeoned but not murdered she continues to sing her song of hope even if you never heard her

And despite the division i still have a vision of a proud cohesive nation who when banned together can accomplish whatever and are bigger than the issues we're facing

We've been battle tested hate infested and our backs are against the wall and to put this thing back together again it's going to require us all

And although right now it seems impossible don't throw in the towel too soon because those same words were uttered before we put a man on the moon

All we need is a willingness to let our conscious guide us, your fellow citizens aren't your enemy it's the one who tries to divide us

Sure we have our differences what powerful nation doesn't but what seems impossible to overcome willingness will show it wasn't

See the extremist is the one who will sink the ship just because he can't be the captain but i don't think we would stand idly by as a nation and watch that happen

Our democracy our constitution and even our national
anthem can't be surrendered to a disgruntled few every
time they throw a tantrum

So the job for us is to continue to stand against what we
know is wrong and get back to our core beliefs and the
ideals that made us strong

And this goal of ours is not a fantasy it's something we can
achieve your flame of hope may be burning low but for me
i still believe

Going home

I was talking to my boss one day at work and it was just
before the holiday break we spoke about changes coming
about and quotas he wanted to make

But when i asked him what his plans for the holiday was
there was an instant change in tone his face lit up with a
boyish grin and he said to me i'm going home

And without hesitation he begin to go on about the things
that he wanted to do like helping dad with the tree because
of his bad knee and making sure that his brother helped too

He would talk about buddies who still lived in town and
how they all like to still get together what his mother would
make and all of the things she would bake and how they all
had to wear ugly sweaters

He would talk about the town and how they all came
around to partake in the christmas parade and how when
night time came all of his nephews and nieces would all get
together and play charades

I listened to this man go on and on and i can tell that he
held this sacred but there was something nagging at my
mind that i couldn't define and for some reason i just
couldn't shake it and for some reason i just couldn't
shake it

It was my perception of going back home and just how
different my vision might be in a place called home where
the the lawless roamed and all the different characters to see

But just like him at one point in time going home for
me would have been good but unfortunately mine had
a definite decline when they removed neighbor and just
called it hood

Where cats get high and bullet shells fly and sirens are the
background music where kids lock their doors before they
did chores cause if you run up in their spot they got to
use it

Where snitches get stitches and nobody seen nothing was
the doctrine that was written by a hoodlum where you
couldn't tell the cops what was happening on the block
cause you had to be sure that the cop was a good one

Because it's all about green in the land of yameen but it
doesn't mean that christmas wasn't special just keep your
head on a swivel don't get caught up in the middle cause if
cat's catch you slippin they gone test you

Where silent nights just didn't feel right cause it always feel
like someone's out there lurking do you hear what i hear
well you better be clear that means the schemers and the
stick up kids are working

So that's why going back home for me was always somber
and always something different I miss the people the love
the hugs but none of the stresses that went with it

So everything he mentioned only got half attention because
my mind would continue to roam i was jealous of this man
with his joy laced plan Damn i wish i could go home

Summer's Divine

Is it always summer time in heaven or is it also spring
and fall because freezing cold in the streets of gold i can't
imagine at all

But what i can imagine when i think of heaven is a
beautiful summer day bursting with life with birds in flight
where the squirrels and chipmunks play

Where the vegetation is lush & green and the flowers are
bright and vivid cherry blossoms bloom with the scent of
perfume with a backdrop that's esquisite

Where inquisitive butterflies stop to say hi by landing on
your shoulder, fireflies take to the sky when the daytime
shift is over

And a evening spring arise to bring the plants their daily
feeding in a dreamlike scene that's so serene it can only be
described as eden

And in the distance you hear a boisterous cheer as the choir
sings aloud songs of praise as you sit in amaze and fall asleep
on a cloud

This Machine

We've already seen what this machine is capable of doing
the carnage it left the destruction the death the countless
lives it ruined

This soulless faceless diabolical racist manifested in the
form of an ideal uses intimidation, crooked legislation
while convincing you he's not real

It taps into your fears and turn it to hate superseding all
logic & facts with your conscious on hold it takes over your
soul and from this place you react

Using propaganda to belittle and slander because in this state
you;re receptive your common sense and conscious sense all
becomes neglected

All you can see is a fictitious enemy as a threat to your way
of life you no longer see a fellow human being husband,
children or wife

And this so call enemy you see as a threat must be stopped
at any cause even if that means circumventing his rights
civil liberties or laws

You've been told that he's the reason for all the problems
you face and to get what's rightfully yours you must
support the laws that keep him in his place

Media outlets are the tools it use to prepare you for this mission a continuous drive of negative info designed to get you conditioned

All day and all night so you don't lose sight to the point that it becomes subliminal and this persistent voice gives you no choice but to see this man as a criminal

And this pretext used primarily through the news makes you a vital component so when they don't do right and violate his rights it's easier for you to condone it

You know that it's wrong but you just go along with this wicked ideal that's absurd the machine says follow me using mob psychology and your conscious remains unheard

And within this state of blind hate you're capable of the unspeakable gas chambers, bondage, genocide all these things become reasonable

This machine is a constant theme in atrocities throughout the world born in eugenics this immoral menace is the devil himself in pearls

And the misguided fools who follow his rules puts everyone else in danger because they live their lives through mistrust and lies in a perpetual state of anger

Some will see through it and some will not and for them there's no remedy they'll eventually find that they have been blind and that the machine is the only true enemy

The Makeover

Remove your ego, remove your pride and the troubles they
may have brought you, remove religion, doctrine & creeds
that someone else has taught you

Free yourself from external factors that control your every
mood and be cognizant of the diet you choose when
consuming your mental food

Free yourself from seeking acceptance and approval of
someone else then what you do is learn more about you
than the biographies on your shelf

Free yourself from culture ethnicity & race political sides
design to divide and keeping you in your place

Free yourself from people and thoughts that limit your
capabilities that doesn't serve your interest and stunt
upward mobility

These are the things that governed you since the day you
were born and after the removal what you have is yourself
in its truest form

Free of shackles that held you back and made the world
seem frightening now take this brand new shell you have
and rebuild it to your liking

The Black Hole

The black hole has a depthless hole therefore it can never
be full with a continuous hunger to pull you under with its
gravitational pull

Now within that hole it's extremely cold mass,energy,spin
you must continue to fight to get to the light or forever be
trapped within

But the hole plays a integral role and a source of inspiration
that exceeds beyond its event horizon and influences other
nations

Like fashion art, music,lingo things that guide the spirit
influencing those friends & foes and those who fear to go
near it

For those who reside within the hole assimilate into its
culture in the belly of the beast that continues to feast
despite its burning ulcer

Those who try to escape the hole in pursuit of a better
home are pulled back by others even their own brothers for
fear of being alone

But the gravitational pull is so strong that most of them
won't make it some pull their seeds before it feeds and still
they can't escape it

But for those who lives outside of the hole mimic their
characteristics, style of fashion body language down to
their linguistics

But outside remain on high alert when monitoring the hole
fear of spread is what they dread or reversal of the poles

Life outside the hole is great but it can be stressful too
when you're always concern with what's going on and can
it happen to you

Hatred bigotry fear of difference lack of education
fallacious slander propaganda civil rights deprivation

All of these are the actions of an entity without a soul let's
rid ourselves of these toxins now to prevent anymore black
holes

The Devil In The Box

The devil in the box created the plot that the walls are
closing in and despite what they say or even display that
he's your only friend

And that the situation is grim so just listen to him and to
not do so is a mistake and that he's the only one who cares
about you and everyone else is fake

Don't let them distract with logic & facts because that's a
part of their trickery and playing the game of treating people
the same is a road you will find is slippery

And that everyone wants to take from you and everyone
is against you and reasoning is one of their tricks and how
they control your mentals

So only trust those who think like you and those who come
from good stock and don't trust anything you hear unless it
comes from me in this box

Turn me on in the morning before you leave for work, turn
me on when you get in your car turn me on when you get
to your work computer trust me i'm never too far

So when they speak of equality and justice for all you tell
them to go kick rocks i'll be here for you to see you through
sincerely the devil in the box

Beet Cop

When i was a kid growing up where I did we had cops that
walk the beet and this meant periodically throughout the
day there were cops walking down your street

And these cops played a integral role in the community
they weren't like a separate existence and they served and
protect with honor and respect and their presence was
always persistent

Woven into the fabric of the whole neighborhood it made
us feel more connected to us kids they were superheroes
and to our parents they were well respected

And as they made their rounds walking about the town
they allowed some kids to walk with them and if there was
a issue on the block that required a cop you didn't have to
go far to get them

And it wasn't uncommon to see an officer chatting with
your next door neighbor or on your porch with your dad
talking sports or helping him out with a favor

And this relationship we had between one another gave us
a level of trust to point out things we deemed suspicious or
whatever we wanted to discuss

But things got strange when regulations changed and
brought that all to a end where we didn't only lose a
community servant we also lost a friend

The beet cop was gone and life went on but it slowly start
to unravel and what was once concealed was now revealed
as a new foe we had to battle

The dirty deed doers emerged from the sewers in a way that
was cocky and brash and without the beet cop to keep the
streets locked there was no one to take out the trash

Street corners were claimed as they slowly became the base
camp and then the meet spot that couldn't happen before
but they opened the door when the decided to move the beet
cop

And this simple regulation created a barrier between the
cops and our community sure we would see the cops
driving by in there cars but we no longer had the unity

And the level of trust diminished fast as we felt we were
all alone you were more likely to talk to the beet cop then
calling one on the phone

And as time went on the gap got bigger and the barrier
seem to grow higher and as our community was flooded
with drugs the situation became more dire

With no beet cop around to tell what went down calling
was our only go to I'm trusting you with info that can cost
me my life and i don't even no you

Be Like The Tree

Be like the tree that even at birth has to break through the rocky soil and claim your space in whatever you face cause to the victor goes the spoils

Reach to the sky no matter how high when in pursuit of your calling and witness all of the barriers fall like your seasonal leaves when falling

Continue the path after you've done the math and if it's working for you then compound it and if they chose to stay right in your way and you can't break through grow around it

Your objective is clear but not your path and there lies the work that's needed but determination and dedication are the tools required to beat it

When ideas arrive they will start to bud and bloom and their rightful season and not before when they're premature because timing has its reasons

Your branches are kids that grow their own way but share the same roots as their brothers give them room to breath as they sprout their leaves while providing shade for others

So you go on weathering storms but nothing can reach
your core and the summer breeze may rattle your leaves but
your roots remain secure

As you proceed to drop your seeds the process of
germination and in this phase you end your days and make
room for a new generation

Everybody Don't Grow

The natural assumption is as a man grows so does his
maturation and you will see this in the way that he carries
himself and certainly in his conversation

As he grows he receives rewards of patience and pearls of
wisdom so when the youth seek advice on the perils of life
this man will have something to give them

But one shouldn't assume that a person's age and maturation
will definitely align because the one thing we know is
everybody don't grow and you must keep this in mind

Now growth is based on a number of things like your view
of the world and its relation the company you keep the
books you read the level of your education

Life experiences ups and downs all the things you've been
through joy, fears, conquest, tears all of these things within
you

All of these things will culminate in to your ability
to reason like learning permanence doesn't exist and
everything has its season

But for those who don't or should i say won't get stuck in
immaturity and conduct themselves in a childish way and
exposing their insecurities

Quick to argue and become upset because of their rationale
quick to fight because they lack the might to control their
inner child

Negative opinions about everything don't like this or that
more comfortable in crowds of those who are younger
because mentally it's where they're at

So when you're seeking advice from someone older it's
important for you to know to not base it on age alone
because everybody doesn't grow

When You Play Over There

When you play over there the game is different and
different rules apply you didn't see what you know you
seen and you can't be asking why

You kept control while you consoled his mother as she start
to cry and that hurt you more deep in your core than when
you actually watched him die

Everybody around know what went down but on the
streets Mums the word it might seem cruel but that's one
of the rules and i know it sounds absurd

My uncle said this ain't for you it may seem cool but it's not
and it wasn't for your man they found in that van and that's
the reason he got shot

It's it's own world with it's own rules and outside of it
nobody cares but on the inside you will abide when you
decide to play over there

Now for most of us the game's an option but some are
born into it snatched up in their adolescents groomed and
sworn in to it

And for them i pray they find their way because they've
been ill advised governed by a doctrine of self destruction
self hatred and lies

But to those who choose to walk that path it's important
that you understand though even a victim of a unjust
system the blood is still on your hands

And in this role you lose your soul with the toll of death &
despair but these are the consequences you face when you
choose to play over there

Fear Of Death

If we knew exactly what death entailed would the fear of it
subside and when death looms and enters the room would
you try to run and hide

Or do we feel that death is just the end of the physical form
and after you take your final breath your spirit still lives on

And if that's the case then what is it about death that you
actually fear is it leaving behind your family and friends and
people that you hold dear

Or is it things you haven't done but still aspire to do places
you never got to see
Wishes that have yet to come true

Or is it the hell fire you fear that incinerate your sins or
relationships you wanted to fix but never made a menz

Perhaps it's every one of these compounded by the
unknown separation,isolation fear of being alone

The fact that we don't know is the root cause of all our fear,
how will it be ,who will we see, what happens after here ?

The scenarios are endless while these thoughts run through
our mind like what type of legacy are we going to leave
behind

But i don't see death as the end just the beginning of
another story a time to see and reconnect with people that
left before me

A graduation from life on earth celebrating that you
made it where life on earth from your day of birth will be
analyzed and graded

Did you move in the spirit of love or was it strictly wealth
and how close did you actually get to discovering your
higher self

And this answer will determine if they're ready to let you in
or be reincarnated to live a life again

Cause until you reach that level there is nothing you can
bring them because you have to know your higher self to be
worthy of the kingdom

Numb To It

On the news they said a man was found dead and they
followed it up with sports you didn't recognize the name so
it's all the same so you never gave it another thought

A man was found dead with a bullet in his head but bla bla
bla is what you heard cause when there's no connection
then there's no affection so everything else is just words

At one point in time when you heard such a crime if the
tv was on you'd run to it but we've been so infused with so
much bad news that it's now to the point we're numb to it

And it would be unfair to say we don't care because that's
not the case at all we just developed a callous to things that are
malice and what was once big now seems small

And the more we hear the less we hear it's like we're under
the witches spell where headlines change so frequently fast
that we don't have time to dwell

We're so consumed with our daily lives that we don't have
time to run through it
And in order to survive this endless drive we had to become
numb to it

To adapt to your environment is one of life's requirements
and a enate characteristic of man and there's nothing
viscous or even malicious and this part you must
understand

That kane and Able is not just a fable and there's no way
for us to undo it it's just and unfortunate fact that we had
to adapt so that we can become numb to it

Love Vs Hate

Love vs hate is a story we create to suggest some how
they're equal but love fills the universe and encompasses all
while hate only exist within people

See love is bold and blinding like the sun it gives life and
nourishes the living hate hides and try to disguise the
venom and the poison that it's giving

Hate uses trickery and all types of illusions to appear much
bigger than it is by
Snatching the headlines and keeping the people blind to
the beauty that the world has to give

When there's love you will glow when there's hate you are
low and either one will reflect in your demeanor, hate's a
spectator way up in the cheap seats while love would be the
arena

When we see atrocities taking place in the world it really
starts to work on your mind but everyone you see isn't a
product of hate it's just hate leading the blind

A multitude of people and everyone's angry you begin to
think the whole world is evil but that's a trick hate use to
mislead and confuse and the tools that is use to deceive you

But if you were misled and hate screwed with your head
and you went into a evil decent with love in your heart you
can make a new start as the lord for forgiveness and repent

For every ten deeds nine will be good but it's the tenth that
will get the attention
And we know it's not right and that's why it excites and the
reason for your apprehension

So focus on the nine it's the work of the divine and the
deeds we should cherish the most so when we speak of this
state of love versus hate you will see that it's not even close

When Will We See

When will we see that that united we stand but divided
we're destined to fall
And a injustice to them but not to him is still an injustice
to all

And when it's happening over there you really don't care
because everything for you is good until that day it migrates
your way and infiltrate your neighborhood

This divided state that we're living in can no longer be
sustained we shun the mentality of street brutality but
conduct ourselves like gangs

Either you're with me or against me with no in between a
nation divided by views and the primary force for holding
this course is the shit we see on the news

And it permeates every facet of society work, family and
friends and scary when you start to think about how it's all
going to end

We've been driven so far apart from each other that
communication is gone so rely on news and social media
just to know what's going on

Until we find a way to get back to the table and conduct
ourselves like adults with no yelling or screaming or
underhand scheming childish games and insults

Then the threat to our freedom and society as a whole
remains in serious danger while we continue to wait and
operate from a state of selfishness bigotry and anger

A wise man once said that if our nation was to fall or even
be destroyed it wouldn't come from the hand of a foreign
land it would come from the things we avoid

Like dealing with one another in a humane way much
better than we currently do and work as hard as we can to
come up with a plan and stop the prophecy from coming
true

They Didn't Come Home

The downtrodden man is only left with his pride with a
family at home and he can't provide so
They didn't come home
They didn't come home

A dearth of opportunity and less education while dealing
with the harshness of discrimination So
They didn't come home
They didn't come home

Welfare steps in and says we'll give you a hand we can keep
you in this house but you can't have a man So
They didn't come home
They didn't come home

Willing to fight for your country and you're set to deploy
and find the people over there wasn't calling you boy So
They didn't come home
They didn't come home

Hustle dope to support two kids and a wife got caught and
the judge gave you twenty to life So
They didn't come home
They didn't come home

The pressure of society will drive you insane but heroin is a
temporary escape from the pain So
They didn't come home
They didn't come home

It's easy for us to judge and not respect that man but until
you walked in his shoes you just can't understand why
They didn't come home
They didn't come home

Merry Christmas

Behind the hustle the bustle the scuffle and tussle of
checkout lines where insanity prevails because of marked
down sales and shoppers just lose their mind

The spirit of christmas looms above us without a need
to be embellished and it supersede commercial greed and
anything they can sell us

We feel it in our hearts and in our souls as it conjures up
childhood memories of a simpler time we left behind when
everyone seemed so friendly

It almost felt magic and quite surreal full of joy fun and
laughter like a fairytale that wasn't for sale with a happily
ever after

It consumed us all just walking through a mall there was
a joyous intoxication where christmas cheer was in the air
with Santa and decorations

And in the center of town people gathered around while
carolers sing at town hall with hot chocolate eggnog
christmas cookies and everyone had a ball

Kids were giddy with enthusiasm but also conscious
of their mischief because they couldn't risk hitting the
naughty list which meant gettin nuttin for Christmas

And on Christmas eve we all received the rules and how
they apply that if you weren't sleep when Santa came he's
passing your house by

So we rushed to bed and said our prayers bla bla bla my soul
to keep close our eyes and continue to try to force ourselves
to sleep

And when morning came we rushed the tree to verify our
wish list and hear uh uh uh are you forgetting something
i'm sorry Mom Merry Christmas

Man's Need To Know

Go on line and you will find the answer to any question
and if not direct then what you'll get is hypothesis they're
guessing

To be knowledgeable is a powerful thing think,learn,grow
but what you won't see is man's kryptonite I DON"T
KNOW!

To be knowledgeable is to be powerful in some way shape
or form in social circles places of business or educational
forums

Those who possess the knowledge are usually the ones who
run the show and very rarely will you ever hear them say i
don't know

And if they do it's followed up by i will get that answer
to you because to not know is considered a blow to the
competency guru

And we can't have that we need hard facts no theories or
conjectures so when you're in the know and you run the
show it comes with a lot of pressure

And this becomes your makeup and ultimately who you
come to be the one with all the answers who the people
come to see

But that's a hell of a burden for anyone to always be proficient full of pride and playing God and acting as if omniscient

But knowledge is a powerful tool specifically how they use it some sell their souls to keep control and that's why they abuse it

The malicious act of twisting facts with the intentions to mislead used to slander with propaganda and sometimes just for greed

So be certain of the source you seek to be certain they're not pretenders cunning fools with extremist views and pushing their own agendas

You can only sell that and label it as fact to a society that needs to grow predicated on division and headed for collision with man's need to know

At Our Hands

When someone attacks us or treats us unfairly we struggle
to understand we want retribution we want revenge but we
want it to come at our hands

The knee jerk reaction to being mistreated is to respond the
same way they did but that's not how you'll react if slapped
on the back turn around and realize it's a kid

The minute you realize it was a kid that hit you you're
thinking will instantly change you may still get upset
because the kid should know better but it certainly
wouldn't make you deranged

But it's almost the same when dealing with adults and
there's a verbal confrontation you never know what a
person's going through or the troubles they may be facing

See life has a way of working things out and karma plays a
role in that too so when you've been treated in a way you
feel is unfair there's nothing you have to do

But we want gratification we want revenge and we want to
make it hurt cause to just do nothing feel like they got over
but that's just not how it works

There are universal factors beyond our understanding
that governs the spirit of man just trust and believe that
there's really no need for revenge to come at your hands

Schools of Taught

I grew up in a time when people were of the mind that kids
should be seen and not heard fast forward to today just to
hear someone say such a thing would seem absurd

But i also had friends that i grew up with whose households
were a lot less rigid and compared to mine it really blew my
mind and to tell you the truth i just didn't get it

They would talk back to their parents and express their
dislikes and even argue about their curfew but if i talked
back i got slapped and as far as arguing someone would
hurt you

But there were aspects of their life that i really did like
because their home life felt less stressful but there were also
times when dealing with their parents that i personally felt
got disrespectful

But being able to openly express their feelings gave
them a better line of communication because they were
comfortable enough to talk to their parents about most of
their situations

But in absence of that when dealing with your feelings
you basically go at it alone because if you have that rigid
relationship of parent & child you rather deal with things
on your own

But i've seen good and bad come from both schools of
thought so who am i to say which is right if there's not a
firm enough grip there's a chance you can lose them but
you'll crush them if you hold them to tight

Experience VS Hearing

Trying to explain hardship to a child is really a waste of
time expressing your trials and tribulations are equivalent
to nursery rhymes

It's like trying to explain the texture of sand to someone
who's never felt it that's why touching the stove is so
effective because the person actually felt it

Now they may have empathy for what you experienced
and may even be sympathetic but without actually going
through it themselves they really just don't get it

Physical pain or emotional trauma can't be simulated
through words we can design a drone that flies on its own
but it can never mimic a bird

Experiencing things and hearing things can never be one
in the same you sympathize about the oppression that you
learned in your lessons but you really only know it in name

So talk less and listen more when someone's describing
their plight stop bobbing & weaving with all the deceiving
when your not even in the fight

The Road

Everything is about the road and very little of the
destination the journey is to mold and make pieces into
whole and the purpose of our creation

An unaltered life devoid of triumph & strife is a life that yet
to be lived although the road is frightening it is the source
of enlightenment with the pearls & wisdom that it gives

So live life fully and embrace it as it comes because it's all
a part of your maturation don't get too high on the highs
or too low on the lows because they're only temporary
situations

Life at its best is a rigorous test and preparation for your
final exam and that for me is being the best i can be and
truly understanding who i am

Every journey is different every life its own and it's up to
you to find your purpose on the road there will be pain
when finding your lane but in the end it is definitely worth
it

So continue the flow and learn as you go and rely less on
the things you've been told because everything you need in
order to succeed will be taught on this journey called the
road

God & Love

Only love can conquer hate and only god can know your fate but love can also change your fate just as god can also remove the hate

Love is the most powerful force on earth unseen but always felt the power of god is always present and most seeked in need of help

Love can take you to your highest peak and drop you in the lowest valley God can bless you abundantly and leave you with what you can carry

But even dropped in a valley or stripped of your riches it's still considered a blessing you must be calm and patient enough to understand the lesson

So if god is love and love is god they only differ in term then God is in every one of us and love is how we discern

So knowing that the power of love exist inside of you take your lover's hand and look in their eyes and say i'm so in God with you

Where I Wanna Be

In a recliner laid back sipping my favorite Cognac with
a fresh rolled cigar in my hand umbrella propped to give
some shade while listening to the crashing waves,
My feet halfway buried in the sand

Watching people as they walk by a gentle breeze a clear blue
sky as seagulls practice nose dives in the surf at this specific
place and time this piece of heaven is mine all mine and
there's no place i'd rather be on earth

The makings of a perfect day feel the mist of ocean spray
as i give my cigar ash another tap parasailers take to the sky
their pretty colors they're pretty high but i'm perfectly fine
exactly where i'm at

This getaway was my gift to me and there's nowhere else i
wanna be as i start to adjust my recliner further back i wish
this day would never end but i feel the cognac kicking in so i
think i'll take this time to take a nap

Train To Success

All aboard the train to success form the line right here
anyone with carry on excuses check your bags in the rear

Now when i say you must have talent i'm not saying it to
be a jerk and you must also present the proper documents
proving you did the work

In addition you must have tenacity and confidence in what
you do because rejection is inevitable and you must keep
pushing through

Now a good attitude will take you far much further than
gimmicks & tricks i've seen plenty of people with loads of
talent rejected because they were pricks

Now the talent you have is yours alone so don't compare
yourself to others god gives us all a special talent and it's up
to you to discover

So if you're ready then climb aboard this is where your
journey starts but don't even bother coming aboard if you
don't feel it in your heart

None Of These Things Will Matter

Towards the end of your run when it's all said and done
and you're in a moment of deep contemplation you'll start
to reflect on all the boxes you've checked and fulfillment of
your aspirations

Places you've been with family and friends and the
memories that you created memorable events like birthdays
and weddings and the very first person you dated

How much you made or how much you paid on your way
up the corporate ladder may be good for some but in the
days to come none of these things will matter

Disagreements and confrontations are enough to drive us
apart and when it happens with people we love it weighs
heavy on our hearts

And to keep rehashing it in our minds only seems to make
us sadder so turn the page cause in the coming days none of
these things will matter

All we can do is try our best to live a life of virtue and
apologize to anyone if my ways or actions hurt you

And for your sake i hope you take these words as praise or
flatter and get to a space or happier place where none of
these things will matter

The Transition Of Power

When i was a kid growing up where i did there was a time
honored structure that no new phase or passing trend or
new ideal could rupture

Where parents adults and community elders governed the
whole community and it was that mutual respect that kept
us in check and the cornerstone of our unity

See kids and adults had their respective places and very
rarely was that line ever crossed and if a kid found himself
in a room full of adults you can best believe he was lost

Now this power structure we all shared in gave us a sense of
order where any adult could put you back in line you didn't
have to be their son or daughter

It was like a whole community of aunts & uncles and we
all felt somewhat connected and when an adult told you
something you had to do you just did what they said and
respect it

If they were entering a door you held it open, needed a
seat then you got up and if they were engaged in adult
conversation you wouldn't dare interrupt

And this power they had made everything work and made
us better human beings we had self respect and respect for
others just based on the things we were seeing

This was our way and also our culture and we all played
a role within it but things got deranged and everything
changed during the crack cocaine epidemic

We went from fans who played ball to grams & eight balls
and i always had to know who was behind me like the flick
of the living dead where chicks was given head and at night
time the streets filled with zombies

And they would walk all night steal and even fight and for
the drugs they would do the unspeakable but what was
hard to understand is that is that within that clan were
people who were recently teaching you

We seen parents of friends and next of kins and it was hard
to find a family unaffected the crisis no one told you with
the effects of chernobyl and it seemed like nobody want to
check it

For some there was the grave while others became slaves
the beginning of the end of our community and during
this calamity of utter pure insanity the youth seeked out
opportunity

They became entrepreneurs while stumping out the poor
and adding to the ongoing slaughter it was our darkest
hour in the transition of power as they implemented new
hood order

Where the youth was revered respected and even feared
cause of the new found power they poses ill prepared to
lead motivated by greed surrounded by followers who
knew less

A recipe for disaster with no ever after some may even call
it genocide they go to war for blocks sometimes even with
cops and it's hard to imagine the men that died

Such a tragic story to be robbed of your glory when
aspirations and dreams get devoured i would have loved
to see who we would come to be before the transition of
power

Don't Judge

Plenty of times i remember saying there's no way i'd do that
and if it was me they did that to this is how i would react

And everything i said at the time was how i truly felt no
bragging or boasting or doing the most in tightening up
my belt

See it's common for us to speak on things we personally
didn't go through and without thinking twice we give
advice on what a person should do

But life has a way of teaching us to be mindful of our
tongue because some things you swore you wouldn't do
you'll find that you have done

When you said you wouldn't do those things you were
adamant and sure until those set of circumstances came
knocking at your door

Because until you personally experience it it's hard for you
to judge but you're obstinate in what you think so it's hard
for you to budge

But the greatest teacher of all is life and the lessons never end
and instead of being judge & jury it's better to be a friend

So lend a ear to a friend in need and try not to hold a
grudge put down your gavel and remove your robe and
don't be so quick to judge

Wait To Be An Adult

When i was young i couldn't wait to grow up and be an adult
to do what i want when i want with no one else to consult

Because in my my mind being grown was a sign of ultimate
freedom i can come home late even leave the state no more
curfews cause i don't need them

But in the transition from child to adult the responsibilities
differ certainly you can do what you want now that you're
an adult but the consequences are stiffer

Let's say as a child you receive an allowance so you have to
be smart on how it's spent but as an adult you have to focus
your attention on childcare mortgage or rent

The cost of food the cost of crude and saving for kids tuition
child care health care and everything else i'm missing

And christmas time is no longer the same you're not giddy
with anticipation you know exactly what's under the tree
because you have the credit card statement

And staying up late sure you can you can go into 2 in the
morning but it will be a problem at the 8 AM meeting
when you're nodding off and yawning

So trust me kids you're just not ready and don't take it as
an insult enjoy your youth while you still have it and wait
to be an adult

The Other Side

Imagine life on the other side reminiscent of a life that's
past the effects you had on other people's lives and things
within your grasp

Would you be proud of the life you lived and the people
that you inspired or will you fret with total regret that leave
a lot to be desired

But consider this how you see life now will be different on
the other side you won't see things through a negative lens
like jealousy
 envy or pride

Your thoughts will align with the great divine with love and
empathy for all and there will be an affection and a deep
connection to all creatures large & small

You will finally see all the questions you had the answers
reside in the spirit but being bogged down by worldly
sounds made it hard for us to hear it

So we go through life from sermon to sermon dogma,
doctrines & creeds trying to navigate the road to save our
soul from the clutches of deception and greed

Preoccupied with props & lies in search of our salvation
we're told do this and don't do that and if we do then face
Damnation

But on the other side this all subsides as you evolve into pure energy where the spirit of love encompass you like a glove and there's no such thing as a enemy

Where you will take the time to reflect on things you feel you could have done better like a little more patience and understanding and bringing people together

So the task at hand is to take command of this life without ego or pride so in retrospect there will be no regrets when you view it from the other side

Human Interaction

human interaction is fading fast in fact in in a downhill
spiral we learn of one another through network news or the
latest video that's gone viral

We shop online because there's no line and they'll even take
it back if there's an error and between self check out and
ATM's you'll be lucky if you even see a teller

We live in our phones so just leave us alone and we rarely
even talk anymore even ordering food can be construed as
rude when we tell them just to leave it at the door

Less interactions feelings and passion and unfortunate
behavior that's increasing and it's such a disgrace and a hell
of a waste of this wonderful life that we're leasing

It must be ruff on a kid living off the grid and a hinder to
their social development because interacting with others
listening and learning is a social skill that's definitely
relevant

Because what we don't know we start to fear and eventually
come to hate so it's imperative that we get in front of this
thing cause we don't have time to wait

The less we deal the less we feel the colder our society
becomes to where we're just numbers separated in piles and
everyone wants to be number one

It's our fear for one another that's the root of the problem and it causing us to be misanthropic and this point gets exploited by the ones who enjoy it and for some they can even make a profit

That's why it's up to us to respect and trust and come together in a way that's constructive because the route we're on is definitely wrong and by anyone's measure is destructive

Content

There's a great power in being content that most of us
will never know we live our lives in pursuit of more and
constantly on the go

But if we took the time to inventory the things we do poses
undoubtedly you'll come to see your good and also blessed

The problem is we see things through a monetary lens and
gauge ourselves by the success of others family & friends

But being content will show you just how little you really
need and also free your mind from stress gluttony and
greed

So reevaluate your wants and needs and put them in your
proper place prioritize time with family and and friends
and the lord's loving grace

Because no matter how much you already have you will
always want some more but being content with what you
have will help you close that door

And help you see things differently like time more better
spent and all these things await you the moment you
become content

The Soldiers Salutation

For all you do to protect our nation it's dignity and it's pride where individuality and personal agendas all get cast aside

You come together for a common goal to protect this shining star your tenacity in your fight for freedom defines just who we are

We owe you a debt we can never pay though you don't seek reimbursement you just continue to grind and hold the line to prove the praise is worth it

We look to you to keep us safe and maintain peace & order from enemies that are far and near and even within our borders

So i take this time to say to you thanks for what you do your dedication and determination always see us through

Your reputation is one of such that no one can refute you we can never pay the debt we owe but we certainly can salute you

Melancholy

Another rainy day what can i say don't want to laugh don't
want to play

Can't say that i'm mad not even a tad just unmotivated and
that feels sad

The spirit of gloom has entered the room don't know it's
purpose no need to assume

But just like moods they come and go just leave it alone
don't disrupt the flow

Joy will return just like the sun along with the smiles the
laughter and fun

But Mr. melancholy will come again just an unwanted visit
from a real bad friend

But this time around you will know what to do just wait
him out until his visit is through

And while your waiting focus on the fun that will return to
you just as sure as the sun

Conformity

I will not conform to societal norms and move through life
like a robot where the've replaced the art with mechanical
parts and the one that dreams have no shot

A life austere dominated by fear where everything is
black or white where they've omit the grey's where the
conscience plays and justice has a chance to fight

There's a script that's written and we've all been bitten to
fall in line and just follow but once you do you will find it
untrue a life unfulfilled and hollow

But those who stand and take full command with the
courage and just disobeyed you will be shunned by the
swarm that continues to conform for the simple fact that
they were afraid to

Life is short and you only live once so you should live it on
your own accord no one has the right to dictate your plight
or plan it as if they're the lord

It's not a matter of being a rebel a hardnose or just being
ornery it's living your life on your own accord and not
giving way to conformity

Celebrity Woes

What is it about celebrity woes that gets some so excited
breaking news or internet rues is more than enough to
ignite it

The scandalous affair was to much to bare so they're calling
off the wedding infidelity is what they're telling me tune in
for more news at 11

Another alleged victim has just came forward bringing
forth new allegations bad news is supposed to bring the
blues but it feels more like a celebration

This just in with a devilish grin ready to report someone's
misfortune we eagerly wait their entire fate but we'll settle
for just a portion

What is it about the rich & famous their accomplishments
& failures that keeps us engaged beyond the stage and all of
their paraphernalia

Perhaps we see ourselves in them or something we aspire to
be admiration infatuation or something of a higher degree

We take it personal when things go wrong cause we feel like
they let us down cause the attachment we have is more than
surface it's actually quite profound

Their ups their downs our smiles & frowns we seem to
move in lock step and if i go to change the channel from
the latest scandal you'll say hold on not yet

We vicariously live our lives through others which makes
us their harshes critic we hold them to a standard that they
can't sustain but for some reason we just don't get it

They're human beings just like us subjected to mistakes &
flaws but when they fall short of our perceptive thought we
change and out come the claws

Build them up to tear them down that seems to be the
common theme perhaps behind the silliness we're just
envious of the fact that they're living our dreams

And in this dream we created a scene with a happily ever after
not one of shame or faltering fame humiliation & laughter

But the fall of the celebrity is not the issue it's more of
how we see ourselves cause if we held ourselves higher it
wouldn't seem so dyer when someone stumbles and fails

But that's self worth that we must explore and that comes
with knowledge of self to turn the focus inward instead of
outward and tap into our spiritual wealth

And then and only then when we see celebrities getting
trashed for the world to see will we start to regret it and feel
more sympathetic and say damn that could be me

A Life Taken

Congratulations it's a baby boy you couldn't wait to hold
him teach him about life and all that comes with it guide
him teach him mold him

Teach him the lessons the manners the blessings the
things you learned as a kid make sure that he knows how
everything goes the same exact way as you did

Try out for the team it's your father's dream for his boy to
make the roster give it your all when you're throwing that
ball cause you're making your dad a proud poppa

Stay away from those girls they will ruin your world you
should find someone like your mama take it from me you
can see mama and i have no drama

Teach him the lessons of adolescents and how to be a good
father give him the knowledge when picking a college but
make sure it's your alma mata

At the graduation party the cops bust in in the middle of
your celebration and charges you for taking a man's life and
having him live to your expectations

A New Project

I'm working on a project called the polarization dome and
by the year 2050 it will be in every american home

Now how it works, it's a headband with a filtration system
that polarizes negative habits and eventually help you kick
them

Let's say you see a person or thing and you think i really
hate that the opposite pole of hate is love so the filter will
just replace that

And let's say you know a person you think is ugly and
always snooty the filtration will make you see them as a
vision of beauty

The same arguments you always have cause they are
stubborn and so are you the filtration will make you better
see their point of view

Now the downside to wearing the dome is people will start
to hate because people like others to share in their hate but
they can no longer make you

So in the beginning it may be lonely for people who have
the band it's gonna take some time to catch on and for
people to understand

But once it does we will finally have the world's Panacea but
until then go get your band catch you later see ya

The Power Of A Woman

The power of a woman is so immense and have been known through the history of time from kings to pharaohs to the common man all have tasted her wine

Documented history all consist of great and powerful men but behind the scenes were the whispering queens they all confided in

At the end of the day when he's ready to lay next to his queen that he longs to hold he will take her potion swim in her ocean and his mind was hers to mold

She operates from the shadows influencing battles but never really had an official title but her seductive ways made her man a slave therefore her input was vital

Never raises her hand she leaves that for a man with the strength and the brute to protect her who will kill another even his own brother in pursuit of tasting her nectar

Empires have fallen and wars have been waged by men willing to give it their all like the pain that consumed the shah jahan when building the taj mahal

Her smile her gaze she touches she plays are the weapons used at her disposal and even if you don't get it you've been studied and vetted long before she chose you

So beware of the power she uses to devour before you even unsheeved your sword you've been subjugated cause you underestimated the most powerful piece on the board

Do You Have The Strength

Do you have the strength to walk the walk and judge me by my heart or will your family & friends be the judge of my sins and eventually drive us apart

Do you have the strength to stand up to those who tell you what they wouldn't do or will you pay them no mind and respectfully decline cause what we have is between me and you

Do you have the strength to lift me up when the world has beaten me down and be my light in the darkest night when no one else can be found

Do you have the strength to confide in me the way i would do to you and live up to our vows because they're ours and nothing can be more true

Do you have the strength to walk away after given all you can give after saying to yourself i've done all i can but this is no way to live

If so then you have the strength...

Don't Go Down There

Your cursed in public ridiculed and called outside your
name your initial response is to retaliate get upset and do
the same

But if you do you've reduced yourself to a level of despair
and my advice to you before you do just don't go down
there

Hold yourself higher than name calling slander and things
below you even more so in dealing in circles of people who
don't even know you

Don't leave your throne for the sticks & stones the peasants
may throw in the air remain on high where the eagles fly
and just don't go down there

See the harshest words can be used in a way that can tear
someone apart but the same words don't mean nothing if
you don't take things to heart

Only you can determine what those words means and
ultimately how they affect you so don't put much stock in
those who knock and people who don't respect you

Disagreements are part of life and trust me you'll have your
share but when you're reduced to a state of anger and hate
just don't go down there

Let Me Go

Since when did you start drinking that i never seen that
before and what's that thing you do with your wrist every
time you start to pour your starting to turn into someone i
don't even know, *i'm not the person i use to be you have to let
me go*

What is all this talk about you're trying to promote your
brand and tossing out these fancy words that none of us
understand and every time your phone goes off you rush
and have to go, *i'm not the person i use to be you have to let
me go*

Why don't you come around no more to hang out with the
guys and when you do you're ready to go i can see it in your
eyes your only there a minute or so and you always have to
go, *i'm not the person i use to be you have to let me grow*

At the root of the tree we're bounded but as branches
we go our own ways some grow high into the sky for the
sunlight and the rays

Some stay in clusters some go sideways and some of them
just stay low but whatever their path it's theirs to choose
and you have to let them go

When I'm Alone

Only when i'm alone do i feel free the restraints are lifted and i can be me
When i'm in the presence of people i know i'm reading the room i'm gagging the flow
I'm conscious of everything i say what i do and how i play
Sometimes my energy is misconstrued as someone detached or out rite rude
But the fact is that's not me at all i just find comfort behind my wall
But when i'm alone my wall comes down my body relaxes and my mind is sound
Anxiety is low and there's peace of mind and tension and stress gets left behind
A walk in the park, my feet in the sand a book that takes me to distant lands
My time alone is precious to me it eases my mind and sets me free
There's only so much i can spend in a crowd where things are busy and people are loud
The constant movement that keeps me alert home,wife,kids,work
Schedules due dates coming events quotas at work it's all intense
But in the back of my mind it's all okay i just need some time to get away
Where peace and tranquility waits for me when i'm alone when i'll be free

Imagine If

Imagine if amidst the daily chaos turmoil and division
the sky went dark and lightning sparked and in it appeared
A vision
It took some time for the haze to clear and for the image
to become full view but when it did people ran and hid
because at this point we knew
That what we were seeing in the sky wasn't something
made of man and this drew fear that the end was near as we
struggled to understand
Life as we knew it had come to a end and nobody knew
what was next no radio waves no communication
telephone,tv or text
All we had was one another and oddly that felt new terrified
by this great unknown and nobody knew what to do
Frantically people seeked out their love ones but there was
no way to call panic ensued in setting the mood as terror
seduced us all
And this went on for two whole days with no clues or
direction all we had was one another and our faith for
protection
But what was scary was our military who usually protects
us from harm great and powerful weapons of destruction
were suddenly all disarmed
All we had was one another as we sat around just waiting
no thoughts of race political views arguments or hating
The stark reality of our mortality is what we all were facing
no popularity or higher salaries or any dreams we were
chasing

But on the third day of disarray came a great and powerful
voice that uttered four words that everyone heard you have
a choice
And this powerful voice that everyone heard spoke in your
native tongue and in our minds we all felt like the end had
just begun
We stood in a trance listening to demands from what
we called omnipotent as he expressed displeasure in full
measure of misanthropy and dissident
He spoke of the human experience and how it was a gift
but also a test he spoke of the spiritual being seeing our
flaws but also our best
All we have is one another is what he said to us there must
be compassion for your fellow man dignity and trust
Care more for the poor than you do for the war because
that is your occupation death & destruction by the hand of
man will lead to your Damnation
And this lecture went on and on about things we take for
granted how we treat one another but also how we treat the
planet
He spoke of this ill behavior and how it can no longer be
sustained the contemplation of annihilation where only the
planet remains
This radiant power made us cower by the intensity of his
voice as he repeated the phrase he said to us YOU HAVE A
CHOICE
Change your ways in the coming days it's imperative that
you heed this call because when i come again it won't be as
a friend it will be to destroy you all

Being Right Isn't Enough

Family Quarles brings us sorrow and touches us deeper
than most when we hold a grudge with the people we love
family & friends that are close
He said this so i said that and if they don't like it then tuff
that's your decree but eventually you'll see that being right
isn't enough
When you felt you were wronged the anger took over you
were hurt and probably cried but as time goes by the anger
diminish and all you're left with is pride
To not reconcile after it's been a while gets harder as time
goes on it's no longer intense but you're sitting on the fence
because you still don't feel you were wrong
As time goes on maybe even years you've been dealing with
some sorta lost you've convinced yourself you're better of
without them but even still it comes with a cost
The good times you shared when things were better
reminiscing about them can be ruff you'll eventually learn
and then come to terms that being right just isn't enough
If they're going to be there then i'm not coming and if they
do then i'm not speaking what's to gain from embracing
the pain and what exactly are you seeking
You'll tell yourself that i'll be fine but deep down you know
it's a bluff if you have to be the bigger person then so be it
because being right just isn't enough

To Belong

To belong is a sense of security it says that you're not alone
because it's better in a pack when you're being attacked
then standing on your own
But that isn't just limited to creatures of the forest or jungle
where things can hurt you we also see this in everyday life
with people in social circles
The high school division is laid out with precision when
you're finding your place in the herd the cool kids are
popular but that's not stopping ya from joining with the
jocks are the nerds
And if you do college to extend your knowledge a fraternity
might be an option where they'll take you in as their new
found friend almost like an adoption
But ther's also the military you might try if you're more of
a person of action where they'll shape the ideals of how you
feel about different political factions
But independent thinking appears to be shrinking and
they're weird to the people who belong where solitude can
be viewed as rude or maybe you're just not strong
So rather it's crips & bloods or dems & repubs the need
to belong is prevalent cause if you don't belong to this or
belong to that it's almost as if you're irrelevant
But stay the course because it's yours and don't abandon
your ideals because if you commit to something just to
belong chances are it isn't real
But the constant pressure to pick a side always seems to
be looming where network news and political fools set
scenarios for grooming

But be careful of that because very little is fact and
most of it is just deceiving you'll be following a cause of
propaganda and flaws and something you don't believe in
A divided state breeds fear & hate on the road to creating
a monster which help fuels the plan of the wicked man
who's mission is to divide & conquer
So even if your thinking doesn't align with the majority
it doesn't mean your thinking is wrong you just have a
different view and that's okay too but don't feel the need to
belong

Escaped reality

War on drugs war on thugs Narco's VS Cartels law & order
strengthen the boarders successful i can't tell
With opioids there's an epidemic but is it one of morality
some abstain despite the pain but for some it's to escape
their reality
There's a pharmacist in every walk of life so don't get
fooled by the suit & tie but in alley way stables they don't
use labels there's a chance you can shoot & die
But let's go beyond the drugs & crime and the empire that
it created the war on drugs is a insurmountable task and
that point can't be overstated
But the end user or should i say abuser whatever term you
prefer can't deal with a vision that's real and rather see life
through a blurr
What's so pressing about your reality that you feel the need
to escape, societal woes the need to fit in or coming to
terms with hate
Whatever it is it's preventing you from putting both feet on
the ground so you fly high through the beautiful sky but
it's still here when you come down
In society's eyes your a criminal loser deadbeat merchant of
sin but that type of talk just provokes you to walk strap in
and take off again
And you continue this cycle until the reaper bites you
or you experience a spiritual break through when you
break through the facade and become one with god and
experience places that the drugs couldn't take you

But the first step is yours and only yours no man or system
can save you
You must break the chain along with the pain of the
substance you became a slave to
So stand up now put your feet on the ground no apologies
or no regrets break down them doors and take back what's
yours and stop playing Russian Roulette

Don't forget to Live

In life we're always planning and when we're not we're
remembering chapters that we've been through or the new
ones that we're entering
Time is our most precious commodity so be careful to
whom you give and in your pursuit of making a living
don't forget to live
i have to do this i have to do that and be finished this by
then but never once did you mention spending time with a
friend
Or taking a walk or reading a book on something that
brings you joy your fondest memories seem to be when you
were a girl or boy
When i retire i'm going to travel and even visit my old town
the question i have for you my friend is what are you doing
now
The destination can be disappointing so maximize the
journey not living life to it's fullest peak is something that
concerns me
So don't waste time with negative minds and people that
are hateful life is a gift and living it well is a way of showing
you're grateful
Work is good and we all should but there also must be
leisure cause none of us gets a second chance to do it like
Ebeneezer
Life is a hour glass and we never know how much sand is
left are you going to live into your twilight years or are you
taking your final breath

So biasly guard your time and space from people and things
that stress us and recognize once it's gone it's gone and
that's what makes it precious
If time is money then you're the teller so be careful to
whom you give and in your pursuit of making a living
don't forget to live

The Sum of Me

If i engage you in conversation then you got to know some
of me but by know means should you assume that that's
the sum of me

And if i did the same to you that would be dumb of me but
i don't see me doing that because that would be under me

Maybe i was projecting an image of someone i wanna be
and if that's the case the reality is you never met none

For the most part i'm a serious guy but there's a funner me
i just don't like to expose it because people make fun of me

Barbequing beer in hand that's the summer me having fun
in the snow that is none of me

Run 3 miles every morning that's the runner me, i don't
run no damn 3 miles look what you've done to me

Trying to impress like i'm the best maybe that's some of me
extremely humble to the point that i mumble that's also
some of me

Loud when i'm right to the point of a fight that is none
of me acquiesce for what i think is best that would be
some of me

These ups & downs and all arounds are what make up the
sum of me on the outside looking in even as a friend you
can only know some of me

Look Up

To look up is a choice we have in any situation even down
in the trenches with life's awful stenches regardless of the
troubles we're facing
The opportunity is always there to see things and see things
different by adjusting your focus from what seems hopeless
can make the world of difference
Look up when things seem down and the weight of the
world is pressing realign your thinking from a ship that's
sinking and put your focus back on your blessings
Because gratitude is a attitude that can change your
spiritual being and change the perspective and possibilities
in everything that seeing
Because to many times when on the grind we lose site of
all the beauty through a strict regiment in the pursuit of
betterment obligation and duty
We consume ourselves with troubles of the world work and
responsibility and very rarely do we stop and ask ourselves
is this the response that's killing
Because beauty ignored is the henchmen's sword that cuts
away life's vitality
That leave us drained and accustomed to pain to where
living is just a formality
Devoid of joy and absence of pleasure while searching for
peace of mind and after years past we finally ask how can i
have been so blind
The choice was always mine to make in how i see things
and how i react we can react from a place of positivity or we
can react from a place of lack glass half empty glass half full

the choice is yours pick one because even if we see it as glass
half empty it's better than a glass of none
But gratitude is such a powerful tool that it puts you in
another class that even if you receive a glass thats empty
you're still grateful that you got the glass but that's another
level of gratification that very few of us have and those who
poses it are consided the blessed and walk on a higher path
above negativity and things that are petty controlling their
moods & emotions like a rock at the shore that continually
endure the punishing waves of the ocean
They remain unmoved and uneasily swayed by the
changing tides of life and where they see lessons and
opportunity most of us just see strife
So keep looking up when things seem down you owe it to
yourself to try to adjust your attire like Earth wind & fire
and keep your head to the sky

Anxiety

Anxiety is a energy we try to control therefore the root of
our discomfort we can suppress it hold it or try to control it
and eventually try to dump it
But the laws of thermodynamics tells us that energy can't
be destroyed we can deny it doubt it or try to reroute but
it's rather hard to avoid
Through your frustration you may ask yourself what the
hells going on inside of me fear plus doubt equals stress and
that opens the door for anxiety
Now the permanent fix is to self analyze and find the root
cause of your stress why are you angry what do you fear
what is it that won't let you rest
But in the meantime when anxiety comes this is all that you
have to do totally relax your body take deep breaths and let
the energy flow through
And at this point you may want to consider partaking in
deep meditation couple this alongside with exercise and
you'll be the medication
Follow these directions that i just gave and everything else
will work out fine and the upside to this prescription i just
prescribe is that my copay is jus $12.99

Life without strife

Life without strife is no life at all to really appreciate life
you must experience a fall

Now the fall can be monumental life changing for sure but
it's happening for a reason and you must endure

Life's throwing you a test you must decipher the code you're
being prepared for something greater further down the road

But you must go through this first and you must do it
alone because on the other side of this lies your thone

Where you'll rule with humility honor ,virtue even forgive
those who spoke ill and tried to hurt you

Because you're a different person now but they don't know
you and that petty bickering is far below you

Mistakes from the past wither away and crumble you're
back where you belong just a lot more humble

Now the mistakes make be gone but the lessons remain
along witht the scars and the emotional pain

But you own it, wear it and conquer it too just as a
reminder of what you've been through

But don't ever forget it even when you stand tall because
without that strife ther's no life at all